11/08

Welcome to France

By Kathryn Stevens

The
**Child's
World**®

Published by The Child's World®
1980 Lookout Drive
Mankato, MN 56003-1705
800-599-READ
www.childsworld.com

Content Adviser: Professor Gichana C. Manyara, Department of Geography,
Radford University, Radford, VA
Design and Production: The Creative Spark, San Juan, Capistrano, CA
Editorial: Emily J. Dolbear, Brookline, MA
Photo Research: Deborah Goodsite, Califon, NJ

Cover and title page photo: Steve Vidler/SuperStock
Interior photos: Alamy: 10 (North Wind Picture Archives), 18 (StockAbcd), 3 top, 19
(David R. Frazier Photolibrary, Inc.), 23 (Robert Harding Picture Library Ltd); Animals
Animals/Earth Scenes: 8 (A. Christof/OSF); AP Photo: 12 (Peter J. Carroll), 20 (Michel
Euler); The Art Archive: 25 (Neil Setchfield); Art Resource: 11 (Erich Lessing); Corbis:
14 (Owen Franken), 15 (Sébastien Désarmaux/Godong); Getty Images: 16 (Chad Ehlers/
Stone), 22 (Nicole Duplaix); iStockphoto.com: 27 (Franck Chazot), 28 (Ufuk Zivana), 29
(Stacey Newman), 30 (Adam Tinney), 31 (Lillis Werder); Jupiter Images: 3 bottom, 21
(SGM/Stock Connection), 24 (Sime s.a.s./eStock Photo); Landov: 26 (Christophe Petit
Tesson/MAXPPP); Lonely Planet Images: 6 (Jean Robert); Minden Pictures: 3 middle, 9
(Cyril Ruoso/JH Editorial); Mira.com: 7 (Galen Rowell); NASA Earth Observatory: 4
(Reto Stockli); Photolibrary Group: 13; Photo Researchers, Inc.: 17 (A. Nicolas/Explorer).
Map: XNR Productions: 5

Library of Congress Cataloging-in-Publication Data
Stevens, Kathryn, 1954–
  Welcome to France / by Kathryn Stevens.
      p. cm.— (Welcome to the world)
  Includes index.
  ISBN 978-1-59296-971-5 (library bound : alk. paper)
  1. France—Juvenile literature. I. Title. II. Series.

DC17.S743 2008
944—dc22

2007034772

Contents

Where Is France? 4

The Land 6

Plants and Animals 8

Long Ago 10

France Today 12

The People 14

City Life and Country Life 17

Schools and Language 18

Work 21

Food 22

Pastimes 25

Holidays 26

Fast Facts About France 28

How Do You Say... 30

Glossary 31

Further Information 32

Index 32

Where Is France?

If you could view Earth from outer space, you would see large land areas called **continents.** One land area is larger than the others. Most of this land area is taken up by the continent of Asia, but the western end is called Europe. France is near the western edge of Europe.

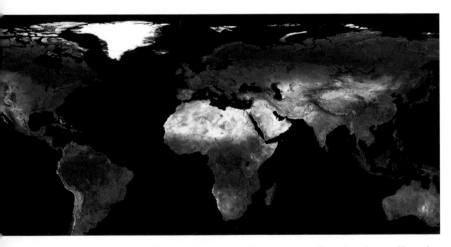

This picture gives us a flat look at Earth. France is inside the red circle.

The Land

France is a land of contrasts. Most of France has broad plains, low hills, and wide valleys and basins. These regions have rich soils for growing crops. The Massif Central in southern France has mountains and rugged, raised "tables" of rock called **plateaus.**

France's Massif Central region covers thousands of square miles.

A climber admires the sunrise in the French Alps.

France has two large mountain ranges called the Pyrenees and the Alps. The rocky Pyrenees form a natural wall between France and Spain. The scenic, snowcapped Alps run through France, Germany, Austria, Switzerland, and Italy.

Plants and Animals

Long ago, most of France was forested. Animals such as deer, wild boars, ibex, and even wolves roamed the woods. Gradually, people turned almost all the forests into farmland. Most of the wild animals died out.

More recently, France has set aside parks to preserve some of its natural lands. Today, about one-quarter of France is wooded, much of it in the parks and mountains. Common types of trees include pine, ash, beech, cypress, olive, and oak.

Did you **know?**

Some of France's flowers, including lavender (below), are grown especially for their scent. Factory workers turn the flowers into expensive perfumes.

8

Wild goats called ibex live in the French Alps.

Long Ago

France has a long, difficult history. The early humans who lived there more than 30,000 years ago left behind stone tools and beautiful cave paintings. By about 2,500 years ago, tribes of Celts (KELTS) ruled France—which was called Gaul at the time. In 58–51 B.C., Julius Caesar and the Roman

Parisians protested against the royal rulers in the French Revolution of 1789.

Empire conquered Gaul. About 500 years later, German tribes called Franks took over. Other peoples, from Arabs to Vikings, also tried to conquer France.

One king after another ruled France. The kings were very rich while the common people were very poor. In the French Revolution of 1789, the common people **overthrew** King Louis XVI and Queen Marie-Antoinette.

In 1799, a brilliant general named Napoléon Bonaparte seized power. Napoléon tried to conquer Europe but was defeated in 1815.

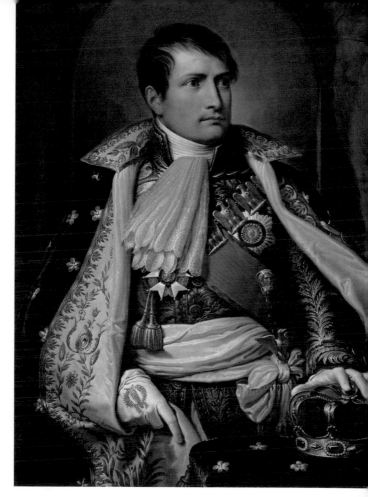

French general Napoléon Bonaparte

11

American troops march down a large avenue near Paris's Arc de Triomphe in 1944.

France Today

In the 1900s, France was at the center of European events. World War I (1914–1918) killed about 1.5 million French soldiers and destroyed many towns. During World War II (1939–1945), Adolf Hitler and Germany's **Nazi** army took over France. A secret movement called the Resistance fought against the Nazis. Near the end of the war, armies from the United States and other countries freed France.

12

Today, France is part of an organization of nations called the European Union (EU). These countries have joined together as business and political partners. The EU even has its own form of money, called the euro. France replaced its money, the French *franc*, with the euro in 2002.

The People

The people of France have different backgrounds. Many French people are related to the invaders of long ago. Other newcomers, or **immigrants,** moved to France from nearby countries such as Italy and Spain.

France is home to many Arabs from North Africa. These French Arab workers serve customers at a fast-food restaurant outside Paris.

More recently, immigrants have come from former French **colonies.** France once ruled colonies in Africa, Asia, and other continents.

More than three-quarters of France's people are Roman Catholics. A much smaller number are Muslim, Protestant, or Jewish. Most Arab immigrants from North Africa and the Middle East are Muslims.

A group of Catholics in Paris gather outside to celebrate Palm Sunday.

15

Buying fresh bread is a daily activity in France's cities and villages.

City Life and Country Life

Parisians enjoy an evening meal at an outdoor restaurant.

More than three-quarters of France's people live in cities. One-sixth live in and around the famous city of Paris. Paris is well-known for its art, literature, music, fashion, and magnificent buildings. Many city dwellers live in apartments. These apartments can be in new high rises or buildings that are centuries old.

The rest of France's people live in the country. Most of them live on farms or in villages. Some farms and villages look as though they have changed little for hundreds of years. Others are more modern.

Schools and Language

A newsstand in Paris

All French children attend school until age 16. Some begin preschool as early as age two. Children go to primary schools to learn reading, writing, and other basic skills. Next they attend secondary schools to learn more advanced subjects. After passing a difficult test, some students go on to universities.

France's official language, French, is spoken around the world. Some people in France speak a dialect, or a local variation, of French. Others speak languages such as Alsatian, Breton, or Basque. These languages and French dialects are most common near France's borders. This is where the languages and customs of the different countries overlap.

These French schoolchildren are on a field trip to see the many cultural sights of Paris, the capital city.

French workers manufacture millions of automobiles each year.

Work

French people work at a wide range of jobs. Many work in offices, shops, or open-air markets. Others work in factories that produce machinery, metals, foods, and other products sold around the world. French airplanes and cars are especially important products.

A much smaller number of people still make a living off the land. Some work as farmers, growing wheat, sugar beets, grapes, potatoes, barley, apples, and other foods. Farmers also raise cattle, chickens, and pigs. Many foods are sold at local markets, and many are sold to other countries.

Pickers harvest and transport grapes to be made into wine in eastern France.

21

Food

French cooking, or **cuisine,** is famous worldwide. French cooks make delicious breads, pastries, cheeses, soups, meats, and sauces. Breads are popular, and so are pastries called *croissants* (kruh-SAHNT). Different regions have their own local specialties. Roquefort cheese, for example, comes from a village in southern France. There it is made and aged in the village's deep caves.

A selection of French goat cheeses

France is also known for its wines, which are sold all over the world. The regions of France called Burgundy, Champagne, and Bordeaux all have types of wine named after them. Grapes are grown and made into wine at **vineyards.**

In France, bread comes in many shapes and sizes.

The Côte d'Azur on the Mediterranean Sea is a popular vacation spot.

Pastimes

In the cities, especially Paris, people like to go to concerts, theaters, museums, movies, and fine restaurants. Sidewalk restaurants called cafés are popular everywhere. People sit in cafés drinking coffee, eating, reading, and visiting with friends.

Did you **know?**

The Louvre (LOO-vrh) in Paris, once an enormous palace, is now one of the world's greatest art museums. On display are some 35,000 works of art, including Leonardo da Vinci's *Mona Lisa*.

French people like outdoor sports, too. Bicycle racing, soccer, rugby, and tennis are very popular. Many people still enjoy *boules* (BOOL), an outdoor bowling game. Along the beautiful beaches of the Mediterranean Sea, people swim and relax in the sunshine. In the mountains, they ski and hike.

The French celebrate their national holiday, Bastille Day, on July 14.

Holidays

French people celebrate a number of holidays. Children receive gifts on Christmas, or Noël, and Easter, or Pâques (PAHK). May 8 is Victory Day, which celebrates the end of World War II. Bastille Day celebrates the "storming" of the Bastille prison in 1789. It is one of the most important events of the French Revolution.

France is known around the world for its rich culture and history. If you visit France, you will find lots of beautiful things, from museums to scenic countryside. You will also find plenty of interesting things to do, from hiking to tasting the country's fine foods. You will never be bored in France!

One of the world's most famous landmarks is the Eiffel Tower, built of iron in 1889.

Fast Facts About France

Area: 211,209 square miles (547,030 square kilometers)—slightly less than the size of Texas

Population: Almost 61 million people

Capital City: Paris

Other Important Cities: Lyon, Marseille, Bordeaux, Toulouse, Lille, and Nice

Money: The euro. On January 1, 2002, the euro became the only money for daily business in countries that are members of the European Monetary Union.

National Language: French

National Holiday: Bastille Day on July 14 (1789)

National Flag: A flag with three equal bands of blue, white, and red. The flag is called the French tricolor.

Head of State: The president of France

Head of Government: The prime minister of France

Famous People:

Napoléon Bonaparte: emperor of the French from 1804 to 1815

Louis Braille: blind inventor

Marie Curie: chemist

Claude Debussy: composer

Charles de Gaulle: president of France from 1958 to 1969

Sieur de La Salle: explorer in America

François Mitterrand: president of France from 1981 to 1995

Claude Monet: painter

Montgolfier, Joseph-Michel and Jacques-Étienne: inventors and balloonists

Louis Pasteur: chemist

National Song: "The Song of Marseille" (*"La Marseillaise"*). It became the national song in 1879.

Ye sons of France, awake to glory,
Hark, hark, what myriads bid you rise:
Your children, wives and grandsires aging,
See their tears and hear their cries,
See their tears and hear their cries!
Shall hateful tyrants mischief breeding
With hireling hosts, a ruffian band
Affright and desolate the land,
While peace and liberty lie bleeding?

CHORUS:
To arms, to arms, ye brave!
March on! March on!
All hearts resolved on victory or death.

O sacred love of France, undying,
Thy defenders, death defying,
Fight with Freedom at their side.
Soon thy sons shall be victorious
When the banner high is raised;
And thy dying enemies, amazed,
Shall behold thy triumph, great and glorious.

Repeat CHORUS

French Recipe*: Crêpes

This recipe is for very thin French pancakes called *crêpes*.

1 cup all-purpose flour
2 eggs
½ cup milk
½ cup water
¼ teaspoon salt
2 tablespoons butter, melted

Mix together flour and eggs in a large mixing bowl. Stir in milk and water slowly. Add salt and butter and beat until smooth. Then heat a lightly oiled frying pan over medium high heat. Pour ¼ cup of batter onto griddle. Tilt pan in a circle so the batter coats the pan evenly. After a minute or two, flip the crêpe carefully with a spatula to cook the other side. Sprinkle with sugar or spread with jam, roll, and serve hot.

Always ask an adult for permission and help when using the kitchen.

How Do You Say...

ENGLISH	FRENCH	HOW TO SAY IT
hello	bonjour	bohn-ZHOOR
good-bye	au revoir	oh reh-VWAHR
please	si'l vous plaît	see voo PLAY
thank you	merci	mehr-SEE
one	un	UHN
two	deux	DEUH
three	trois	TRWAH
yes	oui	WEE
no	non	NOHN

Glossary

colonies (KOL-uh-neez) Colonies are lands ruled by a distant country. France once ruled colonies in Africa, Asia, and other continents.

continents (KON-tih-nents) Continents are large land areas mostly surrounded by water. Europe is the eastern part of an enormous continent that also includes Asia.

cuisine (kwih-ZEEN) Cuisine is a style or way of cooking. French cuisine is famous all over the world.

hexagon (HEX-uh-gon) A hexagon is a shape with six sides. People sometimes call France the hexagon because of its shape.

immigrants (IM-ih-grents) Immigrants are people who move to a country from somewhere else. Many of France's recent immigrants have come from Africa.

Nazi (NAT-see) The Nazi party was a political group that controlled Germany from 1933 to 1945 under Adolf Hitler.

overthrow (oh-vur-THROH) To overthrow means to cause the fall or destruction of. The common people overthrew King Louis XVI during the French Revolution.

plateaus (pla-TOHZ) Plateaus are areas of flat land higher than the land around them. Southern and eastern France have some high plateaus.

vineyards (VIN-yerdz) Vineyards are places in which grapes are grown and turned into wine. France has some of the best vineyards in the world.

Further Information

Read It

Connolly, Sean. *The French Revolution*. Chicago, IL: Heinemann, 2003.

Crosbie, Duncan. *Find Out About France: Learn French Words and Phrases and About Life in France*. Hauppauge, NY: Barron's Educational Series, 2006.

Fontes, Justine and Ron. *France*. Danbury, CT: Children's Press, 2004.

Lethbridge, Lucy. *Napoleon*. London: Usborne, 2005.

Look It Up

Visit our Web page for lots of links about France:
http://www.childsworld.com/links

Note to Parents, Teachers, and Librarians: We routinely verify our Web links to make sure they are safe, active sites—so encourage your readers to check them out!

Index

animals, 8, 21
area, 4
Bonaparte, Napoléon, 11
cafés, 25
education, 18
European Union (EU), 13
farming, 17, 21
food, 21, 22
French Revolution, 11, 27
government, 11
history, 10–13
holidays, 26–27
immigrants, 14, 15
industries, 21
language, 18
Massif Central, 6
money, 13
mountain ranges, 6, 7, 8
Paris, 17, 25
religion, 15
sports, 25
trees, 8
World War I, 12
World War II, 12, 26–27